Home Office Research Study 181

Coroner service survey

by
Roger Tarling

A Research and Statistics Directorate Report

Home Office
Research and
Statistics
Directorate

London: Home Office

Home Office Research Studies

The Home Office Research Studies are reports on research undertaken by or on behalf of the Home Office. They cover the range of subjects for which the Home Secretary has responsibility. Titles in the series are listed at the back of this report (copies are available from the address on the back cover). Other publications produced by the Research and Statistics Directorate include Research Findings, the Research Bulletin, Statistical Bulletins and Statistical Papers.

The Research and Statistics Directorate

The Directorate consists of Units which deal with research and statistics on Crime and Criminal Justice, Offenders and Corrections, Immigration and General Matters; the Programme Development Unit; the Economics Unit; and the Operational Research Unit.

 The Research and Statistics Directorate is an integral part of the Home Office, serving the Ministers and the department itself, its services, Parliament and the public through research, development and statistics. Information and knowledge from these sources informs policy development and the management of programmes; their dissemination improves wider public understanding of matters of Home Office concern.

First published 1998

Application for reproduction should be made to the Information and Publications Group, Room 201, Home Office, 50 Queen Anne's Gate, London SW1H 9AT.

©Crown copyright 1998 ISBN 1 84082 086 1
ISSN 0072 6435

Foreword

Responsibility for the operation of the Coroner Service is shared between HM Coroners, local authorities, the police service and central government departments. The purpose of the survey, reported here, was to take stock of where the service now stands and, on the basis of the data produced, to allow those with responsibility for the service to consider jointly how best practice might be identified and promoted. The survey raised many interesting issues and a Coroner Service Consultative Committee, consisting of representatives of those responsible for the service, has now been established to consider these and other developments which the service will need to address.

DAVID MOXON
Head of the Crime and Criminal Justice Unit
Research and Statistics Directorate

Acknowledgements

I should like to thank coroners throughout England and Wales, Chief Constables, Chief Executives of Local Authorities and their staff who participated in the survey by completing questionnaires and providing invaluable advice and comments. In particular, I would like to record my immense gratitude to Robert Clifford of the Coroners Section of the Home Office for his guidance and support throughout the project.

Roger Tarling

Contents

		Page
Summary		vii
1.	**Introduction**	**1**
	Organisation of the Coroner Service	2
	Aim of the study	3
	Design of the study	3
	Response to the questionnaire	4
	Outline of the report	5
2.	**Coroners & their staff**	**7**
	Administrative staff & coroners' officers	9
3.	**Physical resources and services**	**15**
	Accommodation	15
	Court facilities	17
	Mortuary facilities	18
	Pathology services	19
	Other resources	20
4.	**Costs and workload of the coroner service**	**21**
	Costs incurred by the police service	23
	Financial amanagement	24
	Workload and its relation to costs	26
5.	**Other issues**	**31**
	Professional status and pay	31
	Law and procedure	32
	Training	32
	Coroners' officers	34
	Responsibility for the service	35
	Financial issues	35
References		**37**
Publications		**39**

Summary

The aim of the study was to obtain an up to date picture of the coroner service. Information was sought from coroners of the 148 coroners' districts in England and Wales, from local authorities (who meet the expenses of the coroners in running the service) and from the police service (who provide coroners' officers in most districts).

In any one year about 190,000 deaths are reported to coroners and this number represents about a third of all deaths occurring during the year. Post-mortem examinations are undertaken in about two-thirds of cases to ascertain the cause of death. Inquests are held in 12 per cent of cases.

The coroner service is provided on a local basis; the size and composition of coroners' districts vary greatly from the densely populated urban district dealing with more than 3,000 deaths reported to the coroner each year to the geographically large but sparsely populated rural districts dealing with less than 500 reported deaths each year. This variation has resulted in a variety of organisational arrangements and working practices.

Of the 118 coroners who responded, 26 were full time. Some part-time coroners work as little as one day a week, others as much as four days a week. The overwhelming majority (110) came from a legal background; 18 from a medical background (10 had qualifications in law as well as in medicine). The position was similar for deputies and assistant deputies. Part-time coroners invariably practice as solicitors (or in a few cases as medical practitioners). Twenty-two coroners held positions as coroner, deputy or assistant deputy in another, usually a neighbouring, district.

Most full-time coroners have designated, often purpose-built, offices and courts but many coroners, the part-time coroners in particular, work from home or from the premises of their professional practice.

Coroners (and deputies and assistant deputies) are predominantly male; their average age being 58 years. Each coroner has on average three coroners' officers, who are usually provided by the police service.

In addition to the police, other agencies are also closely involved in assisting or providing services to the coroner; in particular funeral directors, health services, medical practitioners and registrars. Funeral directors transfer bodies to mortuaries, which are invariably located at local hospitals (although 24 districts have public mortuaries). Pathologists are called upon to conduct post-mortems.

The costs of the local coroner service to local authorities is in the region of £38 million per year. Police costs are estimated to be a further £8.8 million giving a total of £46.8 million (or about £250 per death). This figure is likely to be an underestimate as it does not include 'out of hours' police cover and capital expenditure on the part of the local authority.

Of the £38 million local authority expenditure, 68 per cent is spent on transferring bodies (£3m), use of mortuaries (£11m) and pathology services (£12m). Coroners' salaries are £4 million, a further 11 per cent of expenditure.

The survey provided an opportunity for consultees to comment widely. The main points to be recorded were:

- a considerable demand for additional training, including courses to be held on week days

- some concerns about the provision and responsibility for coroners' officers

- the difficulty of financial management by the local authority where fees were fixed by the Home Office or determined by the coroner

- a desire for more discretion in holding an inquest

- concerns about the remuneration and status of coroners

- some debate about where responsibility for the coroner service should lie.

I Introduction

In England and Wales, all violent and unnatural deaths and deaths of which the causes are unknown as well as all deaths of persons in custody must be reported to coroners. It is the duty of the coroner to enquire about the cause of death but it is not the responsibility of the coroner to apportion blame as to the cause of death. In any one year about 190,000 deaths are reported to coroners and this number represents about a third of all deaths occurring during the year. The number of deaths reported has been increasing over the last 25 years from about 130,000 in 1970 or just over 20 per cent of all deaths (Home Office, 1997). The other main function of the coroner is to investigate cases of treasure trove but by comparison this is a relatively small component of his or her work. There are about 50 treasure trove inquests per year.

Responsibility for the operation of the coroner service is shared between HM Coroners, the Home Office, the Lord Chancellor's Department and local authorities. Coroners are independent judicial officers and follow the laws and regulations which apply. The Home Secretary is the 'sponsoring' minister for the substantive law; fixes fees and allowances to witnesses, jurors and pathologists; determines coroners' districts; and, in certain cases, approves the appointment of coroners by local authorities. The Home Office also provides training. The Lord Chancellor is responsible for Coroners Rules and may, if he thinks fit, remove any coroner from office for inability or misbehaviour in the discharge of his or her duty. The local authorities meet all the coroners' salaries and expenses in running the service and, outside London and the metropolitan counties, they appoint coroners without requiring the consent of the Home Secretary. There is no dedicated grant for the coroner service, but local authorities nevertheless receive Revenue Support Grant from central government towards their costs.

In many instances the police, along with other emergency services, will be called to the scene of a sudden death–especially in cases where the death occurred in a public place (for example, as a result of a road traffic accident) or where there appeared to be suspicious circumstances surrounding the death. The police are not called to every sudden death. For example, if a person collapsed at home an ambulance would be called and the person taken to the nearest hospital accident and emergency department.

According to a report by Ashley and Devis in 1992, 60 per cent of deaths reported to a coroner each year are voluntarily referred by a doctor, two per cent by a registrar and the remaining 38 per cent from other sources, mainly the police. Given the initial involvement of the police in many sudden deaths and the duty of the coroner to investigate the cause of death and the circumstances surrounding it, the practice has been long established for the police to provide coroners with cornoers' officers to assist them.

Following a sudden death, the body will need to be taken from the scene to the mortuary and this service is invariably provided by local funeral directors unless it has already been performed by the ambulance service. Many mortuaries are located at hospitals: some public mortuaries are not.

To ascertain the cause of death, the coroner may request a medical practitioner to conduct a post-mortem examination. About 126,000 post-mortems are carried out per year which represents about two-thirds of all deaths reported to the coroner. This proportion has been declining slowly since the 1970s when it was about 88 per cent.

If not satisfied that the cause of death is due to a natural cause the coroner will hold an inquest. The inquest is not a trial but a limited inquiry into the facts surrounding a death. In most cases inquests are held without a jury but there are particular circumstances required by statute when a jury must be called, including if the death occurred in prison or in police custody, or if the death resulted from an incident at work. Inquests are held on about 22,000 deaths reported to the coroner, that is approximately 12 per cent of all deaths reported to coroners. About 900 of these inquests will be held with a jury.

Organisation of the Coroner Service

The coroner service is provided on a local basis and the variety in the size and composition of coroners' districts allied to the judicial autonomy of the coroner has inevitably led to a disparate service. There are accordingly contrasting arrangements in different parts of the country in terms of the facilities and services available, mechanisms of finance and organisational structure. It is not therefore entirely valid to conceive of the coroner service as a single entity but instead as a set of local services. Comparisons between coroners' districts must acknowledge the individuality of the service provided.

At the beginning of 1996 the coroner service in England and Wales was organised into 148 coroners' districts.[1] (Since then there have been some

---

1   In addition there is a seperate coroners' district for the Queen's Household. The district was not included in the study reported here; only those covering geographical areas of the country

further changes brought about by the reorganisation of local government.) Not every coroner's district corresponds to any other administrative boundary, such as local authority area (there were nearly 90 local authorities with responsibility for the coroner service in 1996) or police authority area (there are 43 police services). The organisational pattern of the service varies across the country in that many local authorities have more than one coroner district within their boundaries, most police authorities have more than one coroner district within their boundaries and some coroners' districts straddle more than one local authority boundary or more than one police authority boundary. Each coroner district will have a coroner and a deputy coroner. Many districts will also have one or more assistant deputy coroners.

Coroner districts vary enormously in size and workload, from the densely populated urban district to the geographically large but sparsely populated rural district. The average number of deaths reported within each coroner district is in the order of 1,300 but this ranges from a caseload of just over 5,000 in Nottinghamshire, and over 3,000 in many urban centres, to less than 100 cases in four districts, two in rural parts of Wales, one in Lincolnshire and one in the Isles of Scilly. Half of the coroners' districts deal with less than 900 cases per year. The workload of most coroners' districts does not warrant the need of a full-time coroner (although the Coroners rules require coroners to be on call 24 hours of every day). .

Aim of the study

Apart from annual statistics collected on the number of deaths reported to the coroner, the number of post-mortems and the number of inquests held, little information is collected centrally on the organisation, operation and costs of the coroner service and on the extent of the input of other agencies. The aim of the study was to obtain a detailed and up-to-date picture of the coroner service or, more accurately, the 148 coroners' services in respect of organisation, staffing, resources and costs.[2]

Design of the study

It was decided to seek information in respect of each coroner district even though soliciting information in this way resulted in duplication in some instances. For example, when local authorities and police services covered more than one district, they were required to record similar information in

---

[2] No comparable examination has been undertaken in recent times, The last, rather more comprehensive, examination was undertaken by the Brodrick Committee which considered all aspects of death certification in the late 1960s (Brodrick, 1971).

3

respect of each of those districts. After discussions with representatives of the Coroners' Society, local authority associations and the police, it was agreed to obtain information by means of a postal questionnaire. Their representatives were also consulted about the form of the questionnaire and the wording of the individual questions. The questionnaire was sent to other coroners informally and was formally piloted in Cheshire prior to being distributed nationally during late November and early December 1996. Completed questionnaires were received throughout the first quarter of 1997.

The questionnaire was arranged in sections. The first, to be completed by the coroner, sought information on the background characteristics of coroners and their staff and detailed information on the organisation of the service in the district. The second and third sections were to be completed by the police and the local authority respectively. The police and the local authority were asked more general questions about their relationship with the coroner service and on the costs of the service borne by them. Completion of the questionnaire required close liaison and co-operation between the three parties and the Chief Executive of the local authority (or lead local authority where the district straddled more than one local authority) was asked to co-ordinate its completion and return.

Response to the questionnaire

The response rate was high. The coroners' section of the questionnaire was completed in respect of 118 of the 148 coroners' districts, or 80 per cent (although not every question was answered in every return). The police section of the questionnaire was completed in respect of 123 of the 148 coroners' districts. In terms of the number of police services, 40 out of the 43 police services in England and Wales provided information on all or some of the coroners' districts in their area. The local authority section of the questionnaire was completed in respect of 118 of the 148 coroners' districts, which meant that 69 of the 86 local authorities from whom information was requested supplied information on some or all of the coroners' districts in their area.

It was not always the case, however, that all three sections of the questionnaire were completed. For some coroners' districts one or two of the three parties completed their section of the questionnaire. All three sections of the questionnaire were completed in respect of 108 of the 148 coroners' districts and partial information was received for a further 22 coroners' districts. Looked at another way, no information was received for only 18 coroners' districts.

Outline of the report

The next part (Chapter 2) of the report presents information regarding coroners, their deputies and assistant deputies and their staff. Chapter 3 describes the physical resources and services used by coroners to enable them to carry out their duties. Chapter 4 examines the financial management and costs of the coroner service and how those costs relate to workload. The final section, Chapter 5, examines other general issues raised by coroners, police and local authority representatives who completed the questionnaires.

2 Coroners and their staff

It is the duty of the coroner to appoint a deputy and an assistant deputy and, with one exception, each coroner had a deputy and possibly one or more assistant deputies.

Coroners are predominantly male; of the 118 who responded only two were women. (Since the fieldwork for the study was carried out, two more women have been appointed as coroners.) Women are more likely to be represented among deputy and assistant deputy coroners; 23 out of 182 (13 per cent) for whom information was available were women.

There is no statutory retirement age for coroners, who have a relatively high average age (see Table 2.1), although the need to have five years post-qualification experience[1] means that few coroners are likely to be appointed before the age of 30. Coroners were on average 58 years old, with 47 per cent over 60 years old. The youngest was 39 the oldest 75.

Table 2.1: Age of coroners, deputy and assistant deputy coroners

Age	Coroners		Deputy and assistant deputy coroners	
	Number	Percentage	Number	Percentage
30–39	1	1	18	11
40–49	16	14	59	37
50–59	43	38	53	34
60–69	46	40	17	11
70 and over	8	7	11	7
Total	114	100	158	100
No information	4			24

---

1   Under section 2 of the coroners Act 1988 a coroner must have a five year general qualification, within the meaning of the Courts and Legal Services Act 1990 , or be a legally qualified medical practitioner of not less than five years' standing.

The age distribution of deputy and assistant deputy coroners was different. The average age was 51, there was no one under 30 but 11 were over 70, the oldest being 86 years old.

Not surprisingly given the age profile, as a profession coroners have considerable experience. On average coroners have been in their current post for 11.5 years. Furthermore, just under 80 per cent of coroners said that prior to taking up their current post they had been a coroner, deputy or assistant deputy. Deputies and assistant deputies had less experience, the average time in post being eight years and only one-third had held a post in the coroner service prior to taking up their present post.

The professional qualifications of coroners and deputy and assistant deputy coroners are shown in Table 2.2.

Table 2.2: Qualifications of coroners, deputy and assistant deputy coroners

Qualifications	Coroners	Deputy and assistant deputy coroners
Law	110	166
Medicine	18	22

As can be seen, the overwhelming majority came from a legal background; even out of the 18 medically qualified coroners, 10 had qualifications in law as well as in medicine. The position was similar for deputies and assistant deputies, with six of the 22 medically qualified having a legal qualification in addition.

Only 26 (22 per cent) of the coroners were employed full-time. The average amount of time the remaining, part-time coroners, were engaged on coroners duties was about two days per week; a quarter of those that answered this question reported working one day or less per week with the same proportion working two, three and four days per week. All deputy and assistant deputy coroner posts are part-time.

Given that most posts are part-time it is possible for a person to hold more than one post in the coroner service and/or to undertake other work outside. In fact 22 coroners (19 per cent) held positions as coroner, deputy or assistant deputy in another, usually a neighbouring, coroner's district. The overwhelming majority of part-time coroners, deputy and assistant deputy coroners practised another profession. Those with a legal background were mainly practising solicitors and a few held other judicial posts, such as a member of a tribunal. Those with a background in medicine were engaged as medical practitioners in one form or another.

Administrative staff and coroners' officers

Although arrangements as between full-time and part-time coroners will vary they will generally have administrative or secretarial staff to support them as well as coroners' officers who undertake much of the investigative work.

Ninety-one coroners reported that they had such administrative support staff, usually no more than one or two. These often worked part-time and in 60 cases were employed directly by the coroner, usually through his or her other professional practice. In 26 districts, administrative staff were employed directly by the local authority and seconded to the coroner. This occurred most often where the local authority provided dedicated premises in the way of designated coroners' courts with offices incorporated within the same building.

Coroners' officers

Coroners were asked to record the number of coroners' officers assigned to their district. The information is presented in Table 2.3.

Table 2.3: Number of coroners' officers assigned to coroners' districts

Number of coroners' officers	Coroners' districts	
	Number	percentage
0	11	9
1	29	25
2	38	32
3	13	11
4	8	7
5	6	5
6 to 9	6	5
10 or more	7	6
Total	118	100

From the information it would appear that each coroner has, on average, three coroners' officers to assist them but the majority (66%) have two or less. Not all such coroners' officers will be employed full-time on coronal duties. Some coroners did not have any coroners' officers—arrangements for the provision of coroners' officers are discussed below. The number of coroner's officers obviously varied according to the size of the district; many only had one or two whereas some of the large busy districts had more than ten, the largest complement being 13 in one district.

In most cases coroners' officers are provided by the police and information was sought on the police component of the questionnaire. It was stated above that the police are often called to the scene of a sudden death. However, following initial involvement with the case, arrangements vary between police services in the type of subsequent assistance given to the coroner and the way that assistance is organised and delivered.

In most cases (30 out of the 40 that responded) police services employ designated coroners' officers throughout their area.[2] Here the arrangement is to hand as much of the work as possible to the coroner's officer as quickly as possible. The operational officer at the scene would notify the coroner's officer who would attend and assume all responsibilities: for removing the body, notifying next of kin, taking statements, preparing a report for the coroner and, on the instruction of the coroner, taking charge of all subsequent administrative arrangements (a post-mortem, an inquest if required etc).

Most coroners' officers work 'office hours' although a rota system exists to cover absence through leave or illness (in some cases one or two divisional uniform officers will have been trained and would be abstracted from normal duties to act as coroners' officers when required). If the death occurred 'out of office hours' when the coroners' officers were not on duty, the operational officer would refer the case to divisional command who would then arrange for the necessary and more immediate tasks to be undertaken, including making arrangements for the removal of the body, taking care of personal property, notifying next of kin. A short report would be prepared and the matter handed to the coroner's officer when he or she next came on duty. The coroner's officer would then assume responsibility for all subsequent actions.

If the operational police were not involved in the initial stages but the person was taken to hospital and died there, the medical service would notify the designated coroner's officer directly.

---

2   Four services do not have any dedicated coroner officers and six have dedicated officers only in parts of their area.

Line management arrangements for coroners' officers differ. In many areas coroners' officers came under divisional operational command but it was also the practice in others for responsibility to lie with the administrative support unit or the criminal justice support unit. Hertfordshire police have organised their coroners' officers into two units, each unit serving two coroners' districts. The two units, while located in divisions, report to the Operational Support Department at Headquarters; Some other police services co-ordinate the work at Headquarters coroners' officers within the Metropolitan Police, for example, were the responsibility of the Court Division at New Scotland Yard. In practice, however, the day to day work undertaken by coroners' officers is directed by the coroners.

Two police services, Dyfed Powys and North Wales, reported that they did not have, and never have had, designated coroners' officers. The police in these two areas believe the low volume of work and the wide geographical area covered by them does not warrant designated coroners' officers. In practice in both services, officers who first deal with the sudden death become the coroners' officer for that case. They will prepare reports, take statements and obtain any other relevant information. In North Wales the coroner will inform the divisional administrative office of the date he/she intends to hold an inquest and the division administrative staff prepare the summons to witnesses and any other letters to inform interested parties. The police officer attends the inquest. In these two services the police provide the same range of assistance to the coroner as outlined above, but it is organised differently.

Six police services (Cambridgeshire, Cumbria, Derbyshire, Norfolk, North Yorkshire and Northumbria) have designated coroners' officers in some divisions of the service or in some coroners' districts within their boundary (the main urban centres) but not others. In the geographically large but more sparsely populated rural areas there are no designated coroners' officers; all police officers assume the position as the need arises.

The coroners in Gloucestershire and Nottinghamshire have designated coroners' officers undertaking the full range of duties but these officers are not employed by the police or provided by them. In both cases coroners' officers are employed by the local authority. This arrangement has been in operation since 1983 in Nottinghamshire and since 1989 in Gloucestershire.

In Gloucestershire, cover 'out of office hours' is provided by a private company. Under the agreement the company deals with all cases of natural death where the person is over 18. Cases where unnatural cause of death is suspected or where the person is under 18 are dealt with by the police who liaise directly with the coroner. In Nottinghamshire, coroners' officers deal with telephone enquiries out of office hours but do not attend the scene during this period.

In addition to Gloucestershire and Nottinghamshire, Humberside Police is part way through transferring responsibility for coroners' officer posts to the local authorities within its boundary. The two coroners' officers posts in one coroner's district have recently been transferred; the two posts in the other coroner's district will be transferred in autumn 1997. Avon and Somerset police also reported that Avon local authority employs two coroners' officers to work for the coroner in its district.

Background, recruitment and training of coroners' officers

Excluding Dyfed Powys, North Wales, Gloucestershire and Nottinghamshire, coroners' officers are employed as police officers in six areas, as civilians in 16 and in the remaining 14 there is a mixture of police officers and civilians. In many of these 14 areas the commitment is to full civilianisation which is to be introduced over time as police officers retire or resign. However, although many posts are civilian posts the majority of the post-holders are former police officers. The nature and duties of the post and the knowledge and experience required as set out in the job description inevitably favour police officer applicants. Job descriptions state that familiarity with the legal system is needed or that experience as a police officer is desirable but not essential. Two police services went further and made experience as a police officer essential.

Very little formal training is provided to coroners' officers in the discharge of their duties as coroners' officers—as the majority are ex-police officers it is felt that little formal training is needed. In all cases training is provided 'on the job' by being attached, or 'shadowing' a coroner officer for a period of time, usually the officer he or she is to replace. A short induction course is given to those taking up post from outside the police service which is standard practice with all new recruits to the service.

Ten police services stated that they provided coroners' officers with written guidance on how to perform their duties. In many cases these were fairly short summaries of routine procedures to be followed when dealing with cases of sudden death and were part of standing orders. One or two forces had prepared more detailed reports giving information and guidance on a wider range of issues. The report prepared by Derbyshire police included sections on child abuse and dealing with the media. Warwickshire have produced an informative manual covering additional items such as how to handle cot deaths and how to deal with inquests and select juries. The most detailed manual has been prepared by West Midlands Police. It is about 150 pages in length and provides information on names and contact addresses of coroners, coroners' officers, mortuaries and pathologists and others who may need to be called upon. A brief background and history of the coroners service is presented. There are sections on general procedures and on particular issues such as cot deaths and organ donation. Details of various religious death rites are also presented. There is a section on basic anatomy with an appendix on technical synonyms of lay medical and anatomical terms.

3 Physical resources and services

In the main, local authorities saw their role as supporting the coroner service rather than closely supervising it. Local authorities recognised the statutory independence and judicial function of the coroner and accepted the coroner's autonomy. The local authorities' management responsibilities were thus restricted to making adequate provision for the coroner service and funding the service. Resources and services are considered in this chapter; financial management and costs are considered in the next chapter.

The department with day-to-day responsibility for the coroner service varied between local authorities, in part perhaps reflecting their different organisational structures. In about 12 local authorities, responsibility for the coroner service resided with the Chief Executive's Department, in a similar number of local authorities the Solicitor or Legal Services Department assumed responsibility and in a similar number the Secretary's Department was in the lead. However, there were a few local authorities (no more than five in each case) who placed responsibility for the coroner service within Corporate Services, Fair Trading or Trading Standards, Treasurer, Personnel or Environmental Health or Environmental Services.

Accommodation

Coroners and their staff work from a variety of locations. Most coroners cited more than one location: on average, coroners had two offices. Details of accommodation are set out in Table 3.1 overleaf.

Table 3.1: Type of accommodation used by coroner

Type of accommodation	Number of coroners' districts	Percentage of coroners districts
Home	33	28
Coroners' professional practice	58	50
Coroners' court	22	19
Local authority premises	22	19
Police station	64	55
Hospital	16	14
Mortuary	3	3
Other	3	3

It can be seen that 91 coroners work from home or from the premises of their professional practice (78%) and in some cases from both. Often designated coroners' courts have office accommodation within the same building and 22 coroners had offices located with their court. The same number occupied local authority premises (in the case of eight of them in commercial premises rented by the council). Coroners' officers employed by the police were in the main located at police stations distributed throughout the district, although some were located at hospitals and (in the case of three) at the public mortuary.

Coroners were asked whether they had access to computers and in particular whether they had available to them any programmes specially designed to assist coroners' work. If coroners did have such programmes it was most often the 'Ray Hemingray' programme. (This software has been specially developed by an Assistant Deputy Coroner of that name, for use by coroners.)

Table 3.2: Specialist computer programmes available to coroners

Type of computer programme	Number of coroners' districts	Percentage of coroners districts
Ray Hemmingray programme	36	31
Another programme for coroners	5	4
A standard (non-coroner) programme adapted	9	8

Court facilities

All inquests must be held in public and coroners require premises that can be used as courts. Given the large area covered by many coroners' districts and the desirability of holding inquests near the place of death or in a location convenient for the next of kin, a wide variety of premises were used although some were used very infrequently. Coroners listed on average 2.8 venues that were used as courts. Details are set out in Table 3.3.

Table 3.3 : Type of venue used for court hearings

Type of accomodation	Number of coroners' districts	Percentage of coroners' districts
Designated coroner's court	33	28
Magistrates' court/ Crown court	66	56
Local authority premises	61	52
Coroner's professional practice or office	23	20
Police station	11	9
Hospital	8	7
Other	10	9

It can be seen that 33 districts had designated coroners' courts. The majority were large districts covering conurbations with full-time coroners; court and office accommodation being located within the same building. But some part-time coroners also had dedicated courts, for example, old assize courts within County Hall or premises leased by the local authority for the coroner's use. Extensive use was made of magistrates' courts and many coroners listed more than one—in fact it was common to list all the magistrates' courts in the district which may be used at one time or another. Council chambers and other local authority premises were frequently used. Opening inquests were often held at police stations or at the coroner's practice and occasionally at hospitals. Not only was it more convenient to the parties concerned and avoided the problem of trying to obtain scarce court accommodation but, according to several coroners, a less formal setting was often more beneficial to distressed people than formal court surroundings. The 'other' category included church and village halls.

Mortuary facilities

The arrangements for transferring bodies to the mortuary are shown in Table 3.4.

Table 3.4 : Arrangements for transferring bodies to the mortuary

Type of arrangement	Number of coroners' districts	Percentage of coroners' districts
Undertakers on a rota system	45	38
Undertaker(s) with specific contract	29	25
Undertaker located nearest to deceased	8	7
Other	35	30

In 45 (38%) of the coroners' districts it was the practice to have in place a rota of local undertakers. Unless the family of the deceased requested a particular undertaker the police would contact the undertaker whose 'turn' it was—a turn usually lasting one month.

In 29 districts, the local authority had let a contract to a particular firm or firms of undertakers (there might be several firms under contract in different parts of the area). The contract was usually awarded following a process of competitive tendering and might last for one year. In eight districts, the nearest to the deceased was called. This group included one district that had previously tried a rota system but found it to be unsatisfactory.

The 'other' category comprises coroners' districts where there was no formal agreement or contract. Informal agreements, however, might include a commitment to sharing the work between local undertakers on an 'approved list'. In three coroners' districts, or in part of them, the ambulance service provided the service and in one further district it was carried out by mortuary attendants.

Only 11 coroners' districts did not contain within its boundary a hospital with an accident and emergency department and 29 districts had three or more hospitals with such departments. Most of these hospitals have mortuaries which are used by coroners. Other hospitals, without accident and emergency departments, had mortuaries.

Table 3.5: Type of mortuary facilities available

Type of mortuary	Number of coroners' districts	Percentage of coroners' districts
Hospital mortuary	111	95
Public mortuary	24	21

Table 3.5 shows that the overwhelming majority of coroners use hospital mortuaries, which are owned by the local hospital trust. All but four of the 111 said that there was a charge for using these mortuaries, charges usually being incurred on a 'per case' basis.

Twenty-four coroners also had access to public mortuaries. These mortuaries were owned by the local authority, except two which were owned by hospital trusts.

In only 20 districts did coroners have in place a formal contract for the provision of mortuary facilities.

Pathology services

To ascertain the cause of death the coroner may request a medical practitioner to conduct a post-mortem examination. There is no requirement to use a qualified pathologist, but in practice most coroners do so. In certain circumstances special investigation may be needed—such as toxicology.

In 113 coroners' districts, pathology services were provided by the local hospital, invariably the same hospital where the mortuary is located. Standard post-mortems would be carried out at these hospitals. On average coroners used three to four different institutions or establishments providing pathology services. In addition to the local hospital, 20 mentioned that post-mortems are carried out at the public mortuary. Specialist services, such as histology and toxicology, were obtained from the Forensic Science Service (58 coroners said they used this service) or from a university medical school (28 used this service).

In the majority of areas it was agreed that wherever possible a standard post-mortem would be conducted within 24 hours of the death although it was accepted that at weekends this target might not be achieved. Specialist post-mortems took longer and there was no agreed target for service providers. Some coroners commented that this was a problem and suggested that the cause was the absence of a Home Office registered pathologist in their locality.

Other resources

In the course of their work, especially in establishing the circumstances surrounding the cause of death, coroners stated that they drew on the advice and assistance of many agencies in addition to the services of pathologists. Frequently mentioned were the other emergency services—police, fire and ambulance. Health & Safety and factory inspectors were often cited and were called upon where deaths had occurred at work. Similarly experts on gas, electricity and solid fuels were consulted about deaths in the home. Coroners with coastal districts and those which included waterways mentioned using the coast guards and river authorities in cases where death was caused by drowning. Vehicle inspectors were consulted in regard to road traffic accidents, the RAF and air accident inspectors in regard to air crashes and other groups in connection with particular outdoor activities and pursuits (for example equestrian organisations where death resulted from a riding accident). Coroners may also use the services of dentists to establish identity. Translators may be needed in certain cases.

4 Costs and workload of the coroner service

Each year local authorities in England and Wales are required to submit details of their expenditure to the Department for the Environment, Transport and the Regions (DETR). One item identified is the coroner service. From the returns of those local authorities that are involved with the coroner service (shire counties, metropolitan districts, unitary authorities and London boroughs, but not district councils) it appears that expenditure in the financial year 1995—96 was in the region of £38 million (after making some allowance for the very few local authorities who did not provided an estimate to the DETR). However, only a single figure is given and there is no indication of what items are included or how total expenditure is distributed across the range of individual items. In order to gain a fuller understanding of the costs of the coroner service, the survey sought detailed, disaggregated information.

Detailed financial information was available for 107 coroners' districts. By aggregating coroners' districts which were the responsibility of the same local authority it was possible to compare for 49 local authorities the information they provided on the questionnaire with their return to the Department for the Environment, Transport and the Regions. In each case the two figures were very similar. A further comparison was made by adding the information for the 107 coroners' districts and multiplying this figure by 148/107 to obtain a national estimate. The total for the country was estimated to be approximately £38 million which is the same as the total of the returns to the DETR.

Information on the questionnaire made possible an analysis of how the money is spent. Expenditure incurred by local authorities on different services and facilities is set out in Table 4.1.

Table 4.1: Local Authority expenditure on the coroner service: financial year 1995—96

Item of expenditure	Estimated National Expenditure £000s	Percentage
Coroners' salaries	4,256	11
Coroners' personal expenses/ allowances	722	2
Salaries and fees for Deputies and Assistant Deputies	228	1
Deputies' personal expenses/ allowances	5	0
Coroners' officers salaries	262	1
Coroners' officers' expenses/ allowances	76	0
Salaries of all other staff	1,216	3
Personal expenses of all other staff	38	0
Actual or estimated rent of coroner's office	1,748	5
Costs of running coroner's office	1,216	3
Hiring costs	190	1
Transferring bodies to the mortuary	3,306	9
Mortuary services	10,564	28
Pathology services	11,894	31
Other	2,318	6
Total	38,000	

The percentages shown in the table have been rounded for presentational purposes and are derived from the survey returns. The figures in the expenditure column have been grossed up to equate to the national estimate (by multiplying the percentage derived from the survey returns by £38m).

The data in the table show clearly that the major items of expenditure are coroners' salaries, removal of bodies, the provision of mortuaries, and the fees of pathologists. (Expenditure on the last three items could not be separated by every local authority as in 15 cases an aggregate figure only was provided covering all three categories. The procedure followed was to apportion aggregate expenditure across the three items in the same proportion derived from those who did provide the itemised information.) It can be seen that 'removal of bodies', 'mortuaries' and 'pathologists' together account for £26 million which represents 68 per cent of local authority recorded expenditure. Coroners' salaries are £4.3 million, a further 11 per cent of expenditure. These four items, which account for the vast majority (79%) of expenditure, can also be regarded as fairly accurate and reliable estimates.

The remaining 11 items listed in the table, which together account for 21 per cent of expenditure, need to be interpreted with great care. In many cases a different combination of items of expenditure were subsumed under one payment in the financial returns and it proved impossible to disaggregate the data. For example, some local authorities pay one sum to the coroner to cover the cost of deputies, assistant deputies, support staff, their expenses as well as the costs of accommodation and running the coroner's office. Some coroners have a designated coroner's court with office accommodation incorporated within the same building. In these cases it was difficult for the local authority to separate how much of the expenditure was for the court and how much for the office accommodation. The combined figure was listed under either court cost or office accommodation.

The other limitation of the expenditure on these 11 items is that in many cases they underestimate the true costs. It appears from examination of the questionnaires that some facilities are not charged to the coroner service particularly where they are provided by the local authority, such as the use of council chambers for holding inquests or where the local authority provides accommodation. Local authorities did not make any allowance for the capital costs of providing buildings. The use of magistrates' courts did not always incur expenditure.

Notwithstanding these caveats, the category 'other', which is the more prominent accounting for £2.3 million, includes some office related expenditure such as insurance or software licences but in the main comprises reimbursing witnesses and jurors their expenses for attending inquests (at rates fixed by the Home Office). Three other items incurred expenditure of over £1 million, 'salaries of all other staff', 'actual or estimated rent of coroner's office' and 'costs of running coroner's office'.

The figure for coroners' officers is relatively low because it only includes the costs where the local authority is the employer or meets the direct costs as in Gloucestershire and Nottinghamshire. In other areas the costs of coroners' officers are met by the police.

Costs incurred by the police service

The police were asked to estimate the costs of providing support to the coroner, both the salary costs of coroners' officers and any other costs such as providing out of hours cover, administration and accommodation.

With regard to salary costs of coroners' officers, all 40 police services provided information. However, four do not have dedicated coroners' officers and one other service provided information for only some of the coroners' districts within its area. Of the 35 that provided information for all coroners' districts the Metropolitan Police (because of its much greater size) incurred much higher costs (£2m) than the 34 provincial services. The salary costs incurred by the 34 provincial services totalled £5.7 million, or an average of £167,000. The total salary costs to the police service was estimated to be 38 x £167k + £2m (the cost incurred by the Metropolitan Police) which equals £8.3 million.

Only 16 police services were able to provide an estimate of other, non salary, costs. Between them they recorded costs totalling £181,000 or an average of £11,300. The estimate for the 43 police services is thus about £500,000. This figure is likely to be a gross underestimate as it seems only to include uniforms, equipment and expenses. It does not appear to include out of hours cover or even full cover in the services which do not have designated coroners' officers. Furthermore, it was shown in Section 3 that most coroners' officers employed by the police are located at police stations but no estimate of their accommodation costs were given.

From the information recorded it can be estimated that the minimum cost to the police service of supporting the coroner service is £8.8 million.

If police costs are added to local authority costs the total known costs of the coroner service are in the region of £46.8 million or about £250 per reported death.

Financial management

Most local authorities reported that they held the budget for the coroner service. Under these arrangements invoices would be submitted to the local authority for payment. Twenty-five local authorities stated that the budget had been delegated to the coroner to manage. Even where the local authority retained control of the budget the coroner would often be given an imprest account to meet immediate expenses of jurors and witnesses. This pattern is broadly shown in Table 4.2 which sets out the type of expenditure by the method of payment. It is based on information provided by coroners and relates to coroners' districts.

Table 4.2: Type of expenditure by method of payment: number and percentage of coroners recording the item of expenditure

Type of expenditure	Number of coroners' districts recording the item of expenditure	Reimbursement by local authority	Direct payment by local authority	Imprest account
		percentage	percentage	percentage
Mortuaries	73	4	88	8
Pathology services	95	15	65	20
Removal of bodies	84	10	71	19
Jurors' and witnesses' expenses	84	19	27	54
Travel expenses	34	74	26	0

It can be seen from Table 4.2 that mortuary costs, pathologists' fees and fees to undertakers to remove bodies are much more likely to be paid directly by the local authority. Expenses to jurors and witnesses and travel expenses incurred by the coroner and his or her staff are paid by an imprest account held by the coroner or paid by the coroner who is then reimbursed by the local authority.

Invariably local authorities take the lead in negotiating contracts and agreements with service providers. This was not an issue where court rooms or accommodation were provided directly by the local authority or where public mortuaries were available. In cases where the coroner used his or her own accommodation an allowance would be agreed with the coroner. Remuneration would also be paid if the coroner directly engaged administrative support staff.

All local authorities that answered the question stated that the coroner service was routinely audited by the authority's internal audit department. Three reported that audits had been conducted by the Audit Commission or the District Audit. Relatively few local authorities reported specific exercises aimed at achieving value for money. Nine said that they had competitively tendered contracts for removing bodies (and had achieved substantial savings as a result). Four said that they had compared their costs with those of similar or neighbouring authorities to reassure themselves that their costs were not out of line.

Workload and its relation to costs

Coroners' districts vary enormously in terms of their workload and in the characteristics of the communities that they cover; from the geographically small but densely populated urban areas with a large number of deaths, to the geographically large and sparsely populated rural areas with a small number of deaths. Inevitably these characteristics shape working practices and have a bearing on costs which may also be affected by the different pay arrangements between full-time coroners (paid a salary) and part-time coroners (paid according to the number of cases handled).

For the above reasons, it may not be meaningful to compare widely different coroners' districts or to draw conclusions from such comparisons. It is more appropriate to compare districts similar in size and composition and this formed the basis of the analysis reported here. Coroners' districts were divided into four groups. The first comprised districts with a workload of less than 500 deaths per year and the second those where the number of deaths was 500 or more but less than 1,000. The third group comprised districts with between 1,000 and 2,000 deaths and all those with more than 2,000 deaths fell into the fourth group.

The purpose of the following analysis is to provide a series of average measures, or benchmarks, by which others may judge the cost effectiveness of the service or by which individual coroners or local authorities may reflect on, or compare, their own performance and costs.

Information on the number of post-mortems and inquests was drawn from the annual statistical returns submitted to the Home Office by each coroner. Data for 1995 (Home Office, 1996) are presented in Table 4.3.[1]

Table 4.3: Number of post-mortems and inquests as a proportion of all deaths reported by size of coroner's district: 1996

Number of deaths reported	Post-mortems as a percentage of deaths reported			Inquests as a percentage of deaths reported		
	Average	Minimum	Maximum	Average	Minimum	Maximum
Less than 500 (32 districts)	78	46	100	15	8	25
500 to 999 (52 districts)	70	25	96	13	6	22
1,000 to 1,999 (36 districts)	71	48	97	12	5	25
2,000 or more (27 districts)	64	43	97	12	7	22
Total (147 districts)	68			12		

It can be seen from Table 4.3 that on average post-mortems are requested in 68 per cent of deaths reported. However, a trend is discernible in the data in that the larger the district in terms of the number of deaths reported the smaller the percentage that required a post-mortem. In addition to the overall trend there was considerable variation between districts within each group as can be seen from the 'minimum' and 'maximum' columns.

A similar pattern emerged in the proportion of deaths for which an inquest was held. Overall 12 per cent of deaths led to an inquest and there was an inverse relationship between the size of the district and the proportion of inquests held. There was also significant variation between districts in the likelihood that a death would involve an inquest.

---

1   Data for 1995 were used as this equated most closely to the financial information collected for the financial year 1995-1996. Note, however, that there were 147 coroners'.

From the financial information provided by 107 local authorities (92 of whom could separate expenditure on transferring bodies, mortuaries and pathologists) and the information on workload (summarised in the previous table) a number of unit costs were calculated. These are shown in Table 4.4.

Table 4.4: Average costs per death reported by size of coroner's district: £s

Number of deaths reported	Costs to local authority	Costs of transferring bodies	Mortuary costs	Costs of pathologists *per number of post-mortems*	Costs of transferring bodies + mortuary costs + costs of pathologists
Less than 500	264	29	72	122	191
	(19)	(19)	(19)	(19)	(19)
500 to 999	239	23	73	95	163
	(36)	(32)	(32)	(32)	(36)
1,000 to 1,999	188	15	48	85	128
	(31)	(27)	(27)	(27)	(31)
2,000 or more	175	13	38	104	100
	(21)	(14)	(14)	(14)	(21)
Total	194	16	51	95	123
	(107)	(92)	(92)	(92)	(107)

(The number of coroners' districts from which the estimates were derived are given in brackets)

The first column of Table 4.4 shows the average total cost to local authorities expressed as a rate per death reported. For the most part this is the cost of the coroner service excluding costs of coroners' officers. If police costs of providing coroners' officers are included average costs increase by between £50 and £60 in each of the groups.

It can be seen that cost per death reported decreases quite substantially according to the size of the district, from £264 in districts with less than 500 reported deaths to £175 in districts with a high workload (2,000 or more reported deaths). It would thus appear from the data that large districts are able to achieve economies of scale. The costs of transferring bodies, presumably over shorter distances in many cases (column 2) and the costs of mortuaries (column 3) appear to be lower in large districts. The costs of pathologists, however, do not show the same pattern. This may not be altogether surprising as the Home Office sets a standard national rate to be paid for such services. Part of the reason for the apparent economies of scale may be that many large districts have public mortuaries, dedicated courts and purpose built offices, although whether this results in a cheaper service cannot be determined from these data as local authorities did not include the capital costs of providing such facilities.

The lower costs in larger districts will also reflect the fact that they have relatively fewer post-mortems and inquests compared with smaller districts.

Within each of the four groups of coroners' districts there was considerable variation between individual districts on all measures of unit cost. It would appear that even where districts are similar in all other respects one is able to deliver the service at a lower cost than another; in some cases by a factor of two. Some variation may be due to the accounting procedures adopted and the inclusion of certain costs in one district but not in another. A detailed audit of each authority's accounts would be needed to identify the true source of the variation but this was outside the scope of the present study. Nevertheless, the figures are sufficiently robust and there would be merit in those responsible for individual districts examining their expenditure against the benchmarks given here.

5 Other issues

In the course of the study, coroners and representatives of the police and local authorities were given the opportunity to comment, either to elaborate on the answers given in response to specific questions or to raise other general issues regarding the coroner service. The purpose was not to obtain a consensus or collective view on any particular issue or a prescription for change but more modestly to reflect the various perspectives held across the service and to ensure that the survey did not miss any issues thought to be worthy of record by those consulted.

Professional status and pay

About 15 coroners raised issues relating to the status and standing of the coroner service. They pointed out that coroners had to be available 24 hours a day every day of the year unlike other judicial officers and the coroner comes under much greater media scrutiny than many judges. Demand had increased and there was a greater expectation on the part of the public but this was not reflected in the status of the profession or in the remuneration that coroners received. One felt that the coroner service was the 'poor relation' of the Home Office and that responsibility should be transferred to the Lord Chancellor's Department along with all other judicial officers. Some of these coroners felt that there should be more full-time coroners and a proper career structure in which deputies would be trained to become coroners. Under such a scheme professional development points would be obtained through formal training and work experience leading to a process of accreditation.

Remuneration was inadequate, some felt, and had fallen behind that of other judicial officers and senior local government officials. Inadequate remuneration for their services both led to the low status of the service and was a consequence of it. It also deterred competent applicants until they were near retirement. One said that coroners did not work just for the money but if pay did not adequately reflect the responsibility and the increasing complexity of the job, difficulties would one day be experienced in obtaining good quality candidates. Another thought that methods of reimbursement of office expenditure should be reviewed on a national basis.

Law and procedure

Several coroners addressed aspects of law and procedure which were said to be out of date and in need of revision. A significant number of inquests were felt unnecessary and only served to increase the distress caused to the family and wasted time and money. Particular examples cited were falls in the home and suicides: "Why should a jury inquest be required if someone jumps in front of a train?". In these cases, it was felt, coroners should be given discretion, at the request of the family, to dispense with an inquest and to publish instead a statement of the facts relating to the death. Another example given of where changes might be considered was in respect of the procedure for removal of bodies out of England. Amendments to the Coroners Act 1988 were felt to be needed in order that coroners were not personally liable for costs upon Judicial Review proceedings. It was suggested that no other judicial officer worked under such conditions. One mentioned that the local authority's responsibility in relation to litigation against the coroner was in need of clarification by way of a circular or, if necessary, by legislation.

Training

An issue explored in the survey was the level of training given to coroners, deputy and assistant deputy coroners. Questions sought coroners' views on the adequacy of training to prepare them and their deputies to perform their duties. A substantial proportion of coroners (40%) felt that the amount of training was not adequate.

Coroners were also invited to suggest ways in which training might be improved and just over a half registered their views. The amount and type of training provided was not thought to compare favourably with the training provided to other professional groups. Some coroners, with a background in the law, felt that training should equate to that given to district or circuit judges and mentioned, with envy, the resources available to the Judicial Studies Board in the Lord Chancellor's Department (LCD). A coroner with a medical background pointed out that five days' training a year is considered as a minimum in medicine (and most doctors receive more).

Many felt that a basic three or four day induction course for newly appointed staff was needed. As most became coroners after serving for a period as a deputy or assistant deputy, the induction course should be directed at deputies and assistants, although a further period of induction might be needed for newly appointed coroners in order to prepare them for tasks not normally undertaken by deputies, such as adjudicating in long or complex inquests.

Induction training should cover basic procedures and administration, and information about coronal law, it was felt. Instruction was also required to facilitate comprehension of anatomy and medical aspects relevant to the coroner's work, in particular the causes of death and how causation was interpreted by pathologists. In addition to formal courses, some coroners suggested the need for other, complementary training materials: newly appointed staff should be sent a list of required reading; a 'ring bound' training manual might usefully be developed in which updates and additional information could be inserted to reflect changes in law, practice and medical advances. One coroner suggested a training video which would provide more flexibility in delivering training.

There was much praise for the Home Office courses which provide subsequent training on particular and specialist aspects of the work of coroners. The Home Office has run two weekend residential courses every year since 1984 and more recently an additional series of occasional one-day non-residential workshops. Approximately 50 places are available at each weekend course. The courses are designed to be of practical use to coroners and include presentations on topics such as industrial diseases, road traffic accidents and hospital deaths.

Coroners said that they had attended on average just under four Home Office courses during their career. Only 11 said that they had never attended a course but in many cases that was because they had not been long in post. Not surprisingly, given that they had been in the coroners service for much less time, (and preference is often given to applications from coroners) deputy and assistant deputy coroners had attended on average fewer courses (1.7). There was little evidence that coroners, deputies or assistant deputies had attended any other training courses in connection with their duties in the coroner service.

Although Home Office courses were highly regarded, certain improvements were suggested. It was felt that there were too few courses making it only possible to attend a course once every couple of years—more courses would allow coroners to attend more often. Some even suggested that attendance at certain regular intervals should be compulsory. To supplement weekend residential courses additional one-day non-residential courses, held during the week, would enable more coroners to attend more easily and be less disruptive to domestic arrangements.

At present most lectures are given by other coroners and it was felt that there should be a greater contribution from professional trainers outside the coroner service. Such people may be better equipped to give guidance on finance, administration, management and specialist aspects of the law and of medicine. They could also address general issues of concern such as judicial competence, racial awareness, dealing with the media and bereavement counselling.

For all Home Office courses it would be helpful if those attending could be supplied with background material beforehand.

Another topic frequently mentioned was the need to be kept up-to-date with case law and there was a request to be provided with transcripts of Appeal Court cases affecting coroners. The requirement here was not so much for courses but the need for information to be circulated quickly. The information provided by the Secretary of the Coroners Society, and disseminated in the newsletter produced by the Home Office, was much appreciated but some felt that coroners should receive a publication equivalent to the LCD *Court Business*.

Coroners' officers

Most police services provide coroners' officers and have no plans to change this arrangement. However, it was mentioned above that in Gloucestershire and Nottinghamshire the police do not provide coroners' officers and Humberside is withdrawing much of its support to coroners and transferring responsibility to local authorities. Merseyside Police also reported that it is proposing this course of action.

Leicestershire Police stated that it would be beneficial for coroners' officers to be employed by the local authority and that has been considered on several occasions. It has not been pursued, however, because the Home Office police grant is only available if the coroners' officers are employed by the police authority. Avon and Somerset had also considered a move in this direction but their review concluded it would not be financially or politically possible–at least in the immediate future. One or two others expressed the belief that coroners' officers should be employed by local authorities even though they themselves had no plans to address the issue.

A number of local authorities expressed concern should the police withdraw the provision of coroners' officers. If this were to take place the total costs of the coroner service would become a greater burden for council tax payers than under the current financial arrangements unless police and local authority budgets were adjusted accordingly. One local authority took a different view; now that the police service had left local government, the position of the coroners' officer should be reviewed: "Coroners' officers are an essential ingredient of the coroner service but now that most posts have been civilianised there seems little point in retaining them in the police structure." It was felt that a more cost effective and indeed efficient utilisation of resources would be achieved by coroners' officers being employed directly by the local authority or by the coroner.

While not seeking to change current arrangements, several police services said that the dual management and accountability of coroners' officers, to the police and the coroner, was in need of clarification. There is obviously a tension in some areas about who 'owns' the coroners' officers and who has the final say in directing their work.[1]

Responsibility for the service

One or two local authorities raised some fundamental questions about their responsibility for the coroner service and queried whether the coroner service should remain part of the local government framework. They felt that local authorities had no real 'locus' or expertise in providing court services.

Financial issues

Many of the comments of local authorities involved their responsibility for financial provision. Being an independent judicial function much of the expenditure of the coroner service was determined by others and the local authority had no control over this. Central government set the fee rates without consultation yet the service was expected to operate within a cash limited budget, they stated. One local authority pointed out that the cost of the coroner service had increased well in excess of inflation year on year which goes against the general local government trend. A review of the funding mechanisms for the coroner service was thought to be worthwhile. A reasonable alternative to the current arrangement, one suggested, would be for the service to be funded by direct specific grant aid from the Home Office.

Several local authorities (and some coroners too) pointed out that the costs of mortuaries and pathology services had risen dramatically in the recent past, largely due, it was claimed, to the establishment of trusts which in many areas have a monopoly in providing these services. One authority reported paying at a rate three times that of bordering authorities and twice the national average, but it had been unable to negotiate a reduction to bring the rate into line or establish an element of competition for the services. It was felt that there should be a clearer definition of the local authorities' role in obtaining value for money in order to overcome these difficulties.

---

1   The trend towards civilianisation raises questions about the supply and training of coroners' officers in the future. Some coroners' officers themselves see the need for these issues to be addressed and, with this in mind, have during the course of this study formed the Association of Coroners' Officers for England and Wales. The objectives of the Association are to develop and promote the post of coroners' officer.

One coroner said that for historical reasons he paid a fee to the mortuary technician, a fee to the hospital and another to the pathologist. The total payment, he felt, was too expensive. Another coroner pointed out that he had to pay an annual fee regardless of numbers and this was not an incentive to reduce numbers. One coroner was given to understand that the coroner service in his area subsidised the total cost of each mortuary. It was claimed by another coroner that if the cost rose any higher consideration would be given to the re-creation of public mortuaries, many of which were closed some 30 years ago.

Other financial concerns included the possibility of major expenditure, as might be incurred following a plane crash, where a long and complex inquest was necessary. There was a need to determine rules and guidance with respect of payments for these exceptional inquests as the additional, unexpected, financial provision often had to be found by the local authority— making precise budgeting difficult.

References

Ashley, J. and Devis, T. (1992). *'Death certification from the point of view of the epidemiologist'.* Population Trends, 67, 22-28.

Brodrick, N. (1971). *Report of the Committee on Death Certification and Coroners.* Chaired by Judge N. J. L. Brodrick. Cmnd 4810. London: HMSO.

Home Office (1996). *Statistics of Deaths Reported to Coroners England and Wales, 1995: Supplementary Tables.* London: Home Office Research and Statistics Directorate.

Home Office (1997). *Statistics of Deaths Reported to Coroners England and Wales, 1996.* Home Office Statistical Bulletin 10/97. London: Home Office Research and Statistics Directorate.

Publications

List of research publications

A list of research reports for the last year is provided below. A **full** list of publications is available on request from the Research and Statistics Directorate Information and Publications Group.

Home Office Research Studies (HORS)

165.   **Enforcing financial penalties.** Claire Whittaker and Alan Mackie. 1997.

166.   **Assessing offenders' needs: assessment scales for the probation service.** Rosamund Aubrey and Michael Hough. 1997.

167.   **Offenders on probation.** George Mair and Chris May. 1997.

168.   **Managing courts effectively: The reasons for adjournments in magistrates' courts.** Claire Whittaker, Alan Mackie, Ruth Lewis and Nicola Ponikiewski. 1997.

169.   **Addressing the literacy needs of offenders under probation supervision.** Gwynn Davis et al. 1997.

170.   **Understanding the sentencing of women.** Edited by Carol Hedderman and Lorraine Gelsthorpe. 1997.

171.   **Changing offenders' attitudes and behaviour: what works?** Julie Vennard, Darren Sugg and Carol Hedderman. 1997.

172.   **Drug misuse declared in 1996: latest results from the British Crime Survey.** Malcolm Ramsay and Josephine Spiller. 1997.

173.   **Ethnic monitoring in police forces: A beginning.** Marian FitzGerald and Rae Sibbitt. 1997.

174.   **In police custody: Police powers and suspects' rights under the revised PACE codes of practice.** Tom Bucke and David Brown. 1997.

176. **The perpetrators of racial harassment and racial violence.** Rae Sibbitt. 1997.

177. **Electronic monitoring in practice: the second year of the trials of curfew orders.** Ed Mortimer and Chris May. 1997.

179. **Attitudes to punishment: findings from the British Crime Survey.** Michael Hough and Julian Roberts. 1998.

No. 159, 175 and 178 are not published yet.

Research Findings

47. **Sentencing without a pre-sentence report.** Nigel Charles, Claire Whittaker and Caroline Ball. 1997.

48. **Magistrates' views of the probation service.** Chris May. 1997.

49. **PACE ten years on: a review of the research.** David Brown. 1997.

50. **Persistent drug–misusing offenders.** Malcolm Ramsay. 1997.

51. **Curfew orders with electronic monitoring: The first twelve months.** Ed Mortimer and George Mair. 1997.

52. **Police cautioning in the 1990s.** Roger Evans and Rachel Ellis. 1997.

53. **A reconviction study of HMP Grendon Therapeutic Community.** Peter Marshall. 1997.

54. **Control in category c prisons.** Simon Marshall. 1997.

55. **The prevalence of convictions for sexual offending.** Peter Marshall. 1997.

56. **Drug misuse declared in 1996: key results from the British Crime Survey.** Malcolm Ramsay and Josephine Spiller. 1997.

57. **The 1996 International Crime Victimisation Survey.** Pat Mayhew and Phillip White. 1997.

58. **The sentencing of women: a section 95 publication.** Carol Hedderman and Lizanne Dowds. 1997.

59. **Ethnicity and contacts with the police: latest findings from the British Crime Survey.** Tom Bucke. 1997.

60. **Policing and the public: findings from the 1996 British Crime Survey.** Catriona Mirrlees-Black and Tracy Budd. 1997.

61. **Changing offenders' attitudes and behaviour: what works?** Julie Vennard, Carol Hedderman and Darren Sugg. 1997.

62. **Suspects in police custody and the revised PACE codes of practice.** Tom Bucke and David Brown. 1997.

63. **Neighbourhood watch co-ordinators.** Elizabeth Turner and Banos Alexandrou. 1997.

64. **Attitudes to punishment: findings from the 1996 British Crime Survey.** Michael Hough and Julian Roberts. 1998.

65. **The effects of video violence on young offenders.** Kevin Browne and Amanda Pennell. 1998.

66. **Electronic monitoring of curfew orders: the second year of the trials.** Ed Mortimer and Chris May. 1998.

67. **Public perceptions of drug related crime in 1997.** Nigel Charles. 1998.

68. **Witness care in magistrates' courts and the youth court.** Joyce Plotnikoff and Richard Woolfson. 1998.

69. **Handling stolen goods and theft: a market reduction approach.** Mike Sutton. 1998.

70. **Drug testing arrestees.** Trevor Bennett. 1998.

71. **Prevention of plastic card fraud.** Michael Levi and Jim Handley. 1998.

Occasional Papers

Evaluation of a Home Office initiative to help offenders into employment. Ken Roberts, Alana Barton, Julian Buchanan and Barry Goldson. 1997.

The impact of the national lottery on the horse-race betting levy. Simon Field and James Dunmore. 1997.

Requests for Publications

Home Office Research Studies and Research Findings can be requested, **subject to availability**, from:

Research and Statistics Directorate
Information and Publications Group
Room 201, Home Office
50 Queen Anne's Gate
London SW1H 9AT
Telephone: 0171-273 2084
Fascimile: 0171-222 0211
Internet: http://www.open.gov.uk/home_off/rsd/rsdhome.htm
E-mail: rsd.ha apollo @ gtnet.gov.u.

Occasional Papers can be purchased from:
Home Office
Publications Unit
50 Queen Anne's Gate
London SW1H 9AT
Telephone: 0171 273 2302